LET'S
see

Ancient Greece

by Cynthia Klingel and Robert B. Noyed

Content Adviser: Michael Danti, Ph.D., Research Specialist,
Near East Section, University of Pennsylvania Museum, Philadelphia

Reading Adviser: Dr. Linda D. Labbo, Department of Reading Education,
College of Education, The University of Georgia

Let's See Library
Compass Point Books
Minneapolis, Minnesota

Compass Point Books
3722 West 50th Street, #115
Minneapolis, MN 55410

Visit Compass Point Books on the Internet at *www.compasspointbooks.com* or e-mail your
request to *custserv@compasspointbooks.com*

Cover: The Parthenon, Athens, Greece

Photographs ©: Eye Ubiquitous/Corbis, cover; North Wind Picture Archives, 6, 10, 12, 14, 16; North Carolina
Museum of Art/Corbis, 8; Scala/Art Resource, N.Y., 18; David Lees/Corbis, 20.

Editors: E. Russell Primm, Emily J. Dolbear, and Pam Rosenberg
Photo Researcher: Svetlana Zhurkina
Photo Selector: Linda S. Koutris
Designer: Melissa Voda
Cartographer: XNR Productions, Inc.

Library of Congress Cataloging-in-Publication Data
Klingel, Cynthia Fitterer.
  Ancient Greece / by Cynthia Klingel and Robert B. Noyed.
    p. cm. — (Let's see library)
Summary: An introduction to the history, government, culture, people, and aspects of daily life of ancient Greece
and its pervasive and enduring influence on western civilization. Includes bibliographical references and index.
  ISBN 0-7565-0293-4
    1. Greece—Civilization—To 146 B.C.—Juvenile literature. [1. Greece—Civilization—To 146 B.C.] I.
Noyed, Robert B. II. Title. III. Series.
  DF77 .K55 2002
  938—dc21   2002003039

Table of Contents

EUROPE

Mount Olympus ▲

Aegean Sea

GREECE

Ionian Sea

● Olympia

● Athens

● Sparta

Mediterranean Sea

N
W ● E
S

City-state ●
Mountain ▲
Greek areas

0   40   80 miles
0   40   80 kilometers

What Was Ancient Greece?

The country of Greece is part of the **continent** of Europe. The country is surrounded on three sides by water. Many islands are part of the land of Greece. It also has many high mountains.

People settled in Greece more than 6,000 years ago. The first recorded dates of ancient Greek history go back 4,000 years. At that time, Greece was a powerful and important country.

◄ *Ancient Greece covered much of the area around the Aegean Sea.*

Who Were the Ancient Greeks?

The first group of people in ancient Greece were the Minoans. They were a **seafaring** people who lived on the island of Crete. They were named after King Minos, the **legendary** ruler of Crete.

The next group of people were the Mycenaeans. They lived on the **mainland.** They often went to war. The poems the *Iliad* and the *Odyssey* tell their history.

The last strong group of people in ancient Greece were the Macedonians. Alexander the Great was a famous ruler. He **conquered** most of the civilized world before he died in 323 B.C.

◄ *Alexander the Great was the powerful leader of the Macedonians.*

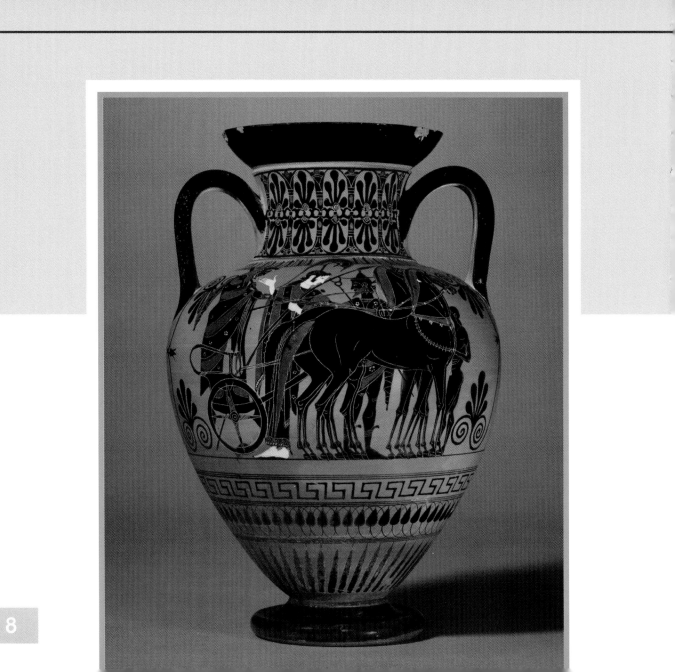

What Was Important to the Ancient Greeks?

Sports and games were important to the ancient Greeks. They liked winning contests. People came from far away to watch their sports events. Not only were sports fun, but they kept the Greek men in good physical shape. This was important because the Greeks often fought in wars.

Art was also important to the ancient Greeks. They enjoyed music and making pottery. Women wove lovely cloth used for clothes and decorating. The ancient Greeks also built very large, beautiful buildings of stone. Some of them are still standing today.

◄ *Ancient Greek pottery was often decorated with beautiful designs.*

What Were the Major Cities in Ancient Greece?

The cities in ancient Greece were city-states. This means the cities were independent and each had its own government. Athens was one of the richest and most powerful cities in ancient Greece. The city of Athens still exists today. It is the capital city of Greece.

Another powerful city in ancient Greece was Sparta. The people of Sparta were known to be brave warriors. The city-states of Athens and Sparta often had disagreements. There were many battles between the two cities.

◀ *The ancient city of Athens*

What Was Life Like for the Children?

Children in ancient Greece played blindman's bluff, tag, and many of the same ball games children play today. Young children played with rattles, dolls, and little toy animals.

Children from farm families worked hard. They had to help on the farm. In the city, boys from rich families had private tutors who taught them at home. Some boys were able to attend school. Girls stayed home and were taught by their mothers. They learned how to take care of a house. They were expected to be good wives and mothers.

Children in ancient Greece played on swings just like children of today.

What Was the Religion of Ancient Greece?

The ancient Greeks worshiped many gods. They believed the twelve most powerful gods lived on top of Mount Olympus. Zeus was the most powerful god. He carried a thunderbolt as a sign of his power over the heavens.

The ancient Greeks worshiped their gods in special buildings called temples. The temples were sacred buildings and believed to be places where gods could live. A statue of a god stood in each temple. An altar outside the temple was used to make sacrifices to the gods.

◄ *The Parthenon was the temple of the goddess Athena.*

What Kind of Work Did They Do?

In ancient Greece, women did the housework. They were expected to make sure there was enough food. They also wove the cloth to make all the clothes. On farms, women also did some of the farmwork. Some homes had servants. The women were in charge of the servants.

Most men in ancient Greece lived and worked on farms. They also went hunting and fishing. War played an important role in the ancient Greek culture. All men were expected to fight with the army.

◄ *Greek women did many household tasks, including needlework.*

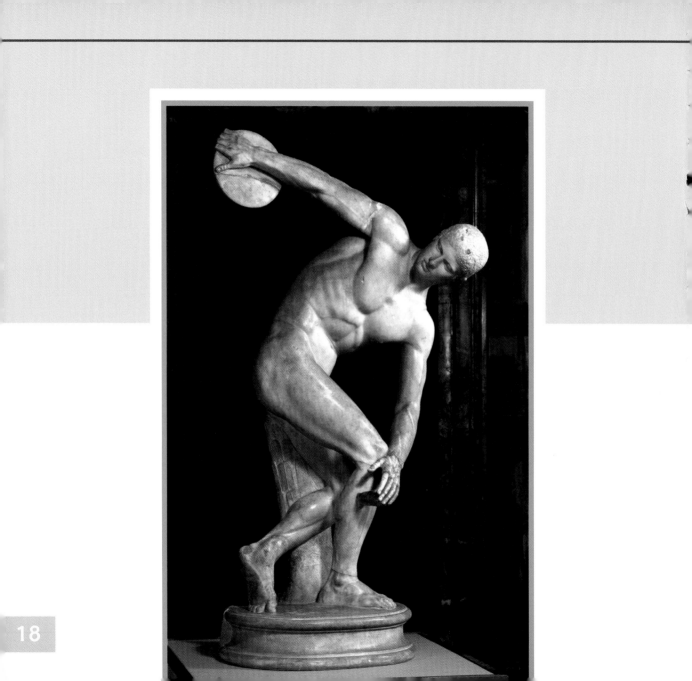

What Are the Olympics?

The most famous sporting event in ancient Greece was the Olympic Games. The Olympics were held in the city of Olympus. They honored Zeus, the king of the gods.

The Olympics were held every four years. The first one took place about 2,800 years ago! One important contest in the Olympics was the pentathlon. It was made up of five separate contests. These were a footrace, the long jump, discus throwing, javelin throwing, and wrestling. The Olympics also included contests in boxing, horseback racing, and chariot racing.

◄ *Discus throwing was one of the contests in the ancient Greek Olympics.*

How Do We Remember Ancient Greece?

We continue to learn about ancient Greece through the work of **archaeologists.** Archaeologists help us learn about life in ancient times. They study the buildings and tools made by the Greeks. These things help us learn how people lived.

Many people still read ancient Greek literature today and view artworks from ancient Greece. Today's Olympic Games remind us of the ancient Greeks, too. Studying ancient Greece can help us understand our modern world.

◄ *Archaeologists open an ancient Greek tomb.*

Glossary

archaeologists—scientists who study people, places, and things of the past

conquered—defeated; overcome by force

continent—one of the large land masses on Earth

legendary—according to old stories

mainland—a continent or part of a continent

philosophers—people who study truth, wisdom, and reality

seafaring—working at sea

Did You Know?

- There were many slaves in ancient Greece. Even the policemen in Athens were slaves. They were called the Athenian archers.
- A healthy body was important to the ancient Greeks.
- Words such as *gymnasium* and *mathematics* come from ancient Greek.
- The ancient Greeks were known for their great thinkers. Socrates and Plato are two ancient Greek **philosophers** whose ideas are still important today.

Want to Know More?

At the Library

Blyton, Enid. *Tales of Ancient Greece*. London: HarperCollins, 1998.

MacDonald, Fiona. *I Wonder Why Greeks Built Temples and Other Questions About Ancient Greece*. New York: Kingfisher Books, 1997.

Pipe, Jim. *Read About Ancient Greeks*. Brookfield, Conn.: Millbrook Press, 2000.

On the Web

Ancient Greece
http://home.freeuk.net/elloughton13/greece.htm
To learn more about the war fought between Athens and Sparta through a story of two families

Daily Life in Ancient Greece
http://members.aol.com/Donnclass/Greeklife.html
To find out more about how the ancient Greeks lived

History for Kids!
http://www.historyforkids.org/learn/greeks/
To learn more about ancient Greece; includes a timeline of Greek history and information on the Olympics

Through the Mail

Embassy of Greece
2221 Massachusetts Avenue, N.W.
Washington, DC 20008
202/939-5800
To write for more information about the country of Greece and its history

On the Road

University of Pennsylvania Museum of Archaeology and Anthropology
33rd and Spruce Streets
Philadelphia, PA 19104
215/898-4001
To tour the Ancient Greek World gallery and view examples of sculptures, coins, vases, and much more

Index

About the Authors

Cynthia Klingel has worked as a high school English teacher and an elementary schoolteacher. She is currently the curriculum director for a Minnesota school district. Cynthia Klingel lives with her family in Mankato, Minnesota.

Robert B. Noyed started his career as a newspaper reporter. Since then, he has worked in school communications and public relations at the state and national level. Robert B. Noyed lives with his family in Brooklyn Center, Minnesota.

T 13974